In *Hawk Parable*, by Tyler Mills, the intricacies of what is seen and what is felt are scars in the body of a bomb survivor or even legacies of guilt. Exposure in the white-hot flashpoints of the atomic age are lessons applicable to now and urgently call us to take heed and notice that "The shadow is an airplane" and that "Vapor is a value." The story of the hunter flying high above the earth is a lesson, also, about the prey and how the exchange between seeing and seen can spell unimaginable horror. The poet traverses the terrain of familial taboo, peering into the past and interrogating what is reflected there in beautiful and painful lyricism.

—**Oliver de la Paz, judge 2017 Akron Poetry Prize**

AKRON SERIES IN POETRY
Mary Biddinger, Editor

Titles published since 2010.

For a complete listing of titles published in the series,
go to www.uakron.edu/uapress/poetry.

Hawk
Parable

Tyler Mills

 The University of Akron Press
Akron, Ohio

Copyright © 2019 by The University of Akron Press
All rights reserved · First Edition 2019 · Manufactured in the United States of America.
All inquiries and permission requests should be addressed to the publisher,
The University of Akron Press, Akron, Ohio 44325-1703.

ISBN: 978-1-629221-05-2 (paper)
ISBN: 978-1-629221-06-9 (ePDF)
ISBN: 978-1-629221-07-6 (ePub)

A catalog record for this title is available from the Library of Congress.

∞The paper used in this publication meets the minimum requirements of ANSI/NISO z39.48–1992 (Permanence of Paper).

Cover image: *Birding*, © Chris Maynard 2017. Used with permission. Cover design by Amy Freels.

Hawk Parable was designed and typeset in Mrs. Eaves with Futura display by Amy Freels and printed on sixty-pound natural and bound by Bookmasters of Ashland, Ohio.

Contents

ʄ

ʄ

ʄ

ʄ

𝔈

𝔈

𝔈

A feather is trimmed, it is trimmed by the light
—Gertrude Stein

Hawk Parable

One morning, a woman had been building shelves for her garage. One of the carpenters helping her brought her a hawk, the feathers glossy as they spread open over her shirt. She noticed the nape: birch-bark white, brown grains in it. This story isn't from a book, though *A Forgotten Past* is tempting.

It hadn't rained in so long the air smelled like crumpled paper.

From a distance, a hawk looks like an eagle. An eagle shows its eye on the back of a dollar bill. She noticed dove feathers—engraving

The vending machine eats them.

gray—from the things that refused to leave her garden. She Googled "hawk eating dove":

Someone made the video by holding her hands very still.

the eye reflects nothing, and sticky feathers cling to the hawk's beak as it hammers at the puffed breast. She watched the video until the dove started breathing

An eye gone black.

the way you might, running down a dirt path, the sun burning shadows out of the ground. The carpenter set the hawk down on the concrete floor,

Make it mean something.

turned away. The woman switched on a band saw. She pulled a 2x4 through the blade. The hawk had been stunned by a car and woke back to itself—

The woman wanted to paint it.

a spirit that hunts the ground. She hoped it would live. She went inside for her camera. When she returned, the bird was gone.

Make it mean.

First Thing

You look like a monster, one woman said to another.
The woman was on fire. This is the first of two
screws twisted into a wall. One bus is sent
on its route minutes before the other. This
is the first. Thousands of soldiers were lowering
their faces to the grass, as though an exercise
can will an effect. People made their way
to the hospital: a doctor would look at them,
and then they could die. You can dip a line
of monofilament into a river. You can do
it twice. The first becomes a second. The second becomes
a third. Three girls stretched out their arms while the wind
sheared their flesh. Sheared, not seared, what was left.
I could have shown you a swimming pool lit with turquoise light.
It was early. It was a mission. It wasn't the first.

The Sun Rising, Pacific Theatre

Here we have another moment of blue-sky thinking,
when no one loves you in the morning.
The tinderbox as empty as a train at 5 a.m.

It is 5 a.m.: a tin knife and fork packed in your pants,
you yank the sheets up where your neck
placed an envelope of nerves.

Acrid sky over us, streaked with the tar
blur of gasoline: the sky knows the machines
are being fed—that is blue-sky thinking,

when no one loves you less. I want to touch the raw
cloth of your coat sleeve while you put your body
inside it: it's like I'm the voice from the beginning

of an opera that speaks from the ceiling
gilded with octagonal tiles to say, *there are exits*
on all sides. But you are moving like a wheel

riding over a rope, and your lover
is your hand, lacing up boots through their rusted portals.
The sky reminds me of nothing, the way it feels

staring into white curls of light combed through stones.
What I thought was a tinderbox is actually
a box of bullets. What you thought was the sun is the sun.

Negative Peeled from a Cardboard Album

For a moment,
soldiers don't cross
the path. My eye

inspects it: three tents
cluster the background.
Morning. Island light:

glare of water, of all
surface. My eye
chooses three

overcoats hanging
loose from a wire:
white shouldered

as though inside out.
Top buttons open
into empty necks.

The wind attracts one,
turns a sleeve slightly.
Officers sleep outside

the frame. Outside,
the planes tick with heat.
There is a snake

bleeding out the mouth.
No. A hose leaks water. Tongue
to teeth, I feel a question come—

The Muse Appears in My Kitchen

Let's unbraid your hair, wet for bed,
and comb it loose. Let's talk like sisters.
See this photo? The pilot half stands—

summer making shadows
of the grains in his cheek.
His uniform pulls tight at the cuffs.

His sister's here, watching him
like a window pushed open, today
letting air in. He looks at us instead:

his eyes hooks
inked with little feathers
of light. *See what I mean?*

his sister seems to say,
unscrewing a jar of pickles.
The runway blurs

at 110 miles per hour,
wheels lifting up above a snowy scar.
The mind silvers, sad.

He's at his mother's house
on leave—where is she? *Mom?*
he worries at the lens. *Mom?*

Hypothesis: an Interview

The 21 crews after 4 months training has been reduced to 15.
—Minutes from the Third Target Committee Meeting, May 1945

One chair in a room of chairs is empty,
but the pilot should not sit.
Describe your bank and turns.

Several others wait in their bunker
playing bridge. Did you doze
during practice runs

from Puerto Rico to Venezuela?
The pilot thinks of the halo
of yellow around the window.

Describe what you feel like alone.
In a metal case. On a metal floor.
Do you have a wife?

The pilot told one girl
his family were farmers, from Utah. . . .
Tell us. What is the difference

between handling a B-17 and a B-29?
The pilot remembers eating
under a coconut tree. We understand

you already almost died
once: inside your glass house.
The right wheel didn't descend—

and the ground came closer,
looked like it would scrape
your skin off.

9

You've done well. But how
about being alone. In the light.
Get ready for the secret of your life.

On the Hawk That Crossed My Path in a Dystopian Landscape

ars poetica

The tube of bone weight in your wing
rises with the air like yeast in brown sugar.
A spasm of feathers darkens into a weave

pulled through with wood grains and white thread.
Are you real? You cross over the car and
highway to land in the film of the sun—

empty beaked. You arrive like an answer
to a question I didn't ask. Once I tried
to weave a poem about a medieval castle

in Eastern Europe with words between the bricks
of redacted documents. Why? In the gardens,
cuffed by claw, five hunting birds fought

leather straps staked in the grass. But one peregrine
seemed stuffed it stood so still. You can see
the castle's ridge of iron all through

the city. I drank down soapy pints
of pilsner and pretended to be the moon.
Consider uranium in cabinets, I spit

like salt water from in my throat, yes,
spit into the sink of the poem. Northwest
of the castle, the material comes from mines

in a forest. I drove through the fern light
green in the trees. My lungs in my ribs
opened and shut in the afternoon

like I could lift off the ground, same as now.
The land buries the thing we made to live
just beyond the imagination, like a god,

and you glide above it, dropping the bones
into bushes of juniper. You disappear
and appear. The sun rises and sets.

Nagasaki

Once, when we visited my grandfather,
he spread his hands over the placemats,
palms up. *This is the plane.* Above the creases
brushed like bird-prints across his fingers,
gray wings balanced, stiff as our angry pet cockatiel.
This is the way my mother tells stories:
pausing to notice the cardinals flashing
like wet paintbrushes in the trees.
This is the plane that rested on my grandfather's hands,
the fragile plastic toy model of a B-29. *This is it.*
He clicked a finger against one wing. Plastic flaps
opened. Its propeller spun itself invisible
while wind argued under its cool dark belly.
They interviewed me to do it. I was there,
in one of the other planes, I remember him saying.
The nose was a bulb of glass, inside:
olive green cloth folded above a fist.
A face blurred behind the sun-scarred window.
This is where I sat. Glass clouded with breath
like peeling swirls of glue fingerprints.
A propeller spun itself invisible. Maybe the B-29s
looked like distant white-fronted geese. Maybe
they looked like silver knives in the clouds.
After it drops, you have to count to four. One.
When you see a bright light, you have to pull out.
Two. Maybe Japan looked like a dreaming child
curled in a blanket. Three. *When we got to four,*
nothing happened. Five. *We thought*
something went wrong. Six. *Wrong?* Seven—
propellers spun themselves invisible; strands of cloud
tissue caught fire—a forest pond at dusk
blackening with birds opening up like hands.

Exposure

This road—
No one goes down it,
    autumn evening.
—Bashō

The Baby

I was hanging the baby's diapers on the balcony
when I noticed
a multicolored parachute
floating in the sky.

~

Roof

The shattered glass of the factory
roof fell on us

like rain. I was fascinated
by its beauty.

Had Been

My mother had been picking eggplant
for lunch in the fields.

~

I held
skull after skull
in my hands.

Looking Up

When the air-raid sirens sounded,
I would run

to the shelter carrying
a piece of matting from my room.

We would crouch in the water
until the all-clear.

After, we would throw
ourselves on the grass,

looking up,
and softly sing songs.

Painting

All I could do was walk
with a bottle of olive oil,
painting wounds
with a brush.

~

Washing

She had been standing
in the front hall.

She had been washing her hands.

Face

An apparition
called my name. Its face

swathed in gauze with holes
left for the eyes, nose, and mouth.

My mother.

To Make

Gloves hung loosely
from the fingertips.

I heard a voice telling us
to make
for the hills.

~

Like

Skin hung down from the chest
like rags.

A woman

with an eyeball dangling
down her cheek.

Signs

It rained harder and harder, rain
mixed with black earth.

The words on the signs
burned away.

I Could Not

I found her tightly wedged
from the chest down

into fallen plaster.
The fires were moving closer.

I could not move her.
I placed my hands together

as if in prayer.
I could not let

myself be burned alive.
Mummy isn't brave enough

to stay and die with you.

Forgive me. Forgive me.
I fled.

Not To

When I went to a public bath
I was told
not to come again.

Exposure

Her flesh flaked off
when I touched her leg,
exposing the bone.

~

Drawers

My brother put the bodies into drawers
from our clothes chests.

Relatives collected the bones.

The Fields

Wild chrysanthemums in the fields
were quivering in the wind.

~

The Vases

The doctors had forbidden the patients
water. I poured it from the spout

of a kettle
into the open mouths.

It was like pouring water into the vases
on graves.

Mask

Black and red—a mask.

I could no longer recognize my face.
My eyebrows and lips

disappeared.

~

The injury
had not reached my heart.

It Is

It is impossible
for me to write
any more.

Forgive me.

Guilt Offering

The goat shall carry all iniquities to an inaccessible region.
—Leviticus

So I kissed a goat on the mouth. I was warned.
I looked too fast into its eyes, both
black stitches. Then I found myself
putting my palms over ridges of fur,
quivering, lash-like, into my fingers.
I smoothed the bones and skin.
I believed in you. I put my lips over
the ear, then a force shoved me under
water—
              O the light, an ode
fingering my hair. A scab
shelled off a cloud pouring
smoke into my mind. Get out.
White goat. You were in the trees.
Now I am in the trees. I keep hearing
what I said: *I made the skull.*
I made the brain. Come, animal
with my voice, I need your mind.

Cloud Cover

Unable to See the Ocean or Fix Position by the Stars
—National Geographic, 1943

When is it time to bomb an island?
When clouds stretch into anvils? Or white veils? Or mare tails?
Windy, dry spells carry the best fire:
the air mass moves like a string mop over the floor.

The clouds will be anvils, or veils, or hair.
Our forces and "the enemy" are publishing handbooks.
An air mass turns like a string mop into the floor
of water named *horse latitudes* by early sailors.

The air force published a handbook on the clouds:
white altocumulus resemble a herd of sheep.
Calm water seems to move with manes of light.
And wooden blocks with streamers carry warnings.

The white altocumulus appeared like sheep on a hill
when aircraft carriers slipped in on an eastward storm.
Blocks with streamers came from the sky, meaning something:
imagine the wind blowing hard enough to strip the trees.

The aircraft arrived through high, scattered clouds.
Movie studios pay to know whether rain will fall.
Will the wind blow hard enough to rustle the leaves?
I can't see the power of it, swirling.

Studios record how rain sounds, hitting the leaves.
We know dry wind carries the best fire. Listen.
A power I can't see is swirling around me.
Tell me. When is it time to bomb an island?

Parachute

Now you must learn to fly without even glancing at the instruments.
—Flying and How to Do It

The color of the water itself

is of three kinds: one seen

on the surface,

a kind of milky bloom;

the next where waves let light

through them—at edge—at edge;

and the third, color

showing change

on an object, its sheen,

seen through the water.

Airman on the Ground

Compiled from my grandfather's letters

It's another beautiful day in Chicago and I haven't a thing to do
except listen to the radio. One window overlooks the lake.
    The lights go on, and I don't know where I am for a second.
In fact, I'm writing this letter at a desk

    while I listen to the radio. One window overlooks the lake.
Take care of my car and see that it doesn't freeze up.
    I'M HAPPY OK. I'm writing you this letter.
Tuesday I'm going for a special test and hope I pass.

    Take care of my car and see it doesn't freeze up.
On the way to the show, I rode in a '42, eight-cylinder, super-special Cadillac.
    If I do ship out I'll let you know—I think it all depends on this test—
but I don't know where or when. Every day, a couple fellows leave,

    and I go to a show. That '42, eight-cylinder, super-special Cadillac
reminds me of "my" car. Ha! So far I haven't received any mail—
    I'm beginning to wonder. Every day, a couple fellows leave.
I talk to beautiful girls & eat in their houses, sleep in hotels.

    What happened to my car? I haven't received any mail. . . .
So come on folks, at least a letter a day.
    I talk to beautiful girls & eat in their houses, sleep in hotels.
I feel great—that's why I'm writing a long letter.

    No mail for two days. Come on. At least a letter a day.
Right now I'm looking at the picture I'm going to send you.
    I feel great—that's why I'm writing a long letter.
I'm going to rent a camera, but I won't make more prints.

Right now, I'm looking at my picture that I'll send you.
I'll keep the negatives, as I may be shipped out any day.
I will rent a camera. I might not make more prints.
I hope I can stay here.

I won't be negative. I may be shipped out any day.
I don't know where I am for a second when the lights go on.
I hope I can stay a little longer.
It's another beautiful day, and I haven't a thing to do.

Dream of Taking the Hypoxia Altitude Test in a Metal Bird

Above 10,000 feet,   the sun strobes my window.
No mask marks my mouth.   First, dizziness—

forgetting to eat is like this: you cut into
a waxen green pepper,   seed confetti all over your fingers

as you keep hollowing out the hollow.   This is another
hunger: in a field of corn,   one stalk contains the soul.

Along the highway,
            a quick
shape dissolves in white-sharp spikes.

First,   I see a pile of tractor tires.
Then, a house without a door.   The fire comes,

appearing from the dirt,   through threads of matted grass,
like water wavering as the sun rakes red over

the tide.   This is a test.   I will keep breathing,

as though I am the neighbor on the floor
below your bed who coughs from the blood in the lungs.

Oxygen Mask

My great-grandfather designed the stealth-bomber.
An early prototype. One of its skeleton blueprints
hung on the wall in our sunroom.
The frame caught our faces
if we stood with our eyes close enough to the razor-blade
wings. My brother taped his own airplane drawings
underneath it: gray B-29s shooting from page
to page. My sister scribbled tornadoes
spinning off an ancestry line. I still draw myself: 2B
pencil cracked at the grip, two sheets
of archival paper, one for truth,
the other, lie. I make my eyes closed. I make
my hair look startled—
brown feathers. I make my mouth open—
thin dark slit, as if carved from cypress. A mask
floats above my body. Smooth inside. Sweat
rubbed into an empty silhouette.

Wilderness Road

The trees appear to hang empty
        key rings—no, numbered coins

nailed at forehead height to measure
        the trail. Where will the road widen

so a plow can force snow there, packed and built
        into the ferns, before turning back?

I run as though I'm leaving you
        where the north air

dips into the lungs
        and trappers might have slept.

Quiet, quiet. Where does it
        come from, the laughter

filtering through the pines like ash?
        I find the end of Wilderness Road a theory,

a paved edge that starts
        over in dirt, forbidden

from December to May
        says a sign. I think of ice

ruts and white static filling in
        slowly between the trunks

the way your knees peak the sheets
        in an impossible posture for sleep,

your blue eyes open through their lashes.
    I catch sight of a pond before it changes,

dividing into green and black
    like quick marks someone made with a brush.

I will wade through the hair below
    the surface of the water striped by wind.

I think I hear a car: it doesn't appear.
    Then I feel the forest shift above me

in the blue to gray traffic
    of far tops of trees.

One theory is this could end
    in vines. I imagine them tethered

to a flower a kayak could drift over.
    This morning, your lips made an *ah*

as though you agreed
    with something inside of yourself.

The surface is not a mirror: I held a paddle
    then pulled and pulled through it.

A few Bud Light cans flash from the ferns.
    Leaf shadows pass over my hands.

I believed in the end of Wilderness Road
    until I found it

doesn't exist: you keep going
    further into the mountain.

Reef

Map is not in my thesaurus.
       Many is uncountable, a crowd.
And mar: mutilate, scar, and stain.

       Map would be inlayed between them—
a plan in detail of the numberless
       bacteria collecting on the skin

of coconut milk swirling in a shell.
       Coral is a kind of skeleton
alive in the sea. It can cut your wrist.

       It surrounds a lagoon. Map
offers a place as though it's owned by water.
       There is no better flag.

Do the math. Draw a circle. A fisherman
       pulling up ink-wet crabs
clinging to a net of hemp rope

       will think it's strange to see the sun
rising in the west. Sea stars. Chart the radius.
       Map will always come before scar.

"Mike" Test

Enewetak Atoll, Marshall Islands

I was going to write about a crescent
of honeydew melon. An artist told me

she paints grids when she isn't
certain how to begin. A grid of steel

stores nuclear fuel below the surface
of pools in temporary rooms

with red railings. I glanced at one image,
then checked my email, my nightshade

tank top wet against the dip in my spine
you might like to touch

and say, *Stop. Have a glass of water.*
There once was a structure three stories tall

built on an island Japan surrendered.
This building was a bomb.

At its center, liquid hydrogen filled a thermos.
We nicknamed it after an angel

appearing in the Bible, the Torah, and the Qur'an.
Or maybe the name could have come

from a football player of the fifties
we might remember on Trivia Night.

I think how hammers strike the thinnest
wires inside a piano. Hard.

Once, we evacuated the coral shore
my grandfather could have flown over —

the typed label of his photo
half torn. The Department of the Interior

Master Plan shows where the people will live.
I swallow vomit after watching

the island wart into an orange bulb. Just before,
birds glanced off the shimmering water.

H-Bomb

We could not calculate directions between Johnson, VT, and Elugelab.

We could not calculate directions between Tokyo, Japan, and Elugelab.

Search nearby, e.g., "pizza."

Your search for "pizza" near Elugelab, Enewetak Atoll, RMI, did not match any locations.

Make sure all words are spelled correctly.

Did you mean Marshall Islands resort?

We could not calculate directions between Marshall Islands and Elugelab.

The blast will come out of the horizon just about *there*.

Welcome aboard the USS Estes.

You have a grandstand seat here to see one of the most momentous events in the history of science.

It is now thirty seconds to zero time.

Know about this place and want everyone to find it?

If the reactor goes, we are in the thermonuclear era.

You are about to add a place that you believe is missing so everyone can find it.

Put on goggles or turn away.

Do not face the burst until ten seconds after the first light.

Enter a place name: [a few dozen neutrons].

We do not support adding a place here.

Refresh.

Enter a place name: [water furred with wind].

Refresh.

Enter a place name: [zero].

Fallout

Two-six, approaching ground zero.
All test islands seem swept clean.

Elugelab is calm.
Nothing there but water

and what appears to be a crater.
Try zooming out for a broader look:

water parrot blue in color.
Fourteen Pentagons

could be comfortable inside the hole.
Sorry.

There is so much more that could have been said.
We don't have imagery.

Starfish Prime Pantone-mime

Starfish Prime detonated in space on July 9, 1962

Monarch orange.
Creamsicle tones.
The purple a chicken bone

pulls off of fat.
The stratosphere has been soaped
ginger and tangerine.

I'll wash until it's clean:
orb orbing another orb
mottling like fruit that wets

your fingers and lingers
like being fucked. Pool marine,
dynasty green—golf this sky

into a hole. Colonial
is a color. So is blue atoll.
How the radio

waves cut out voices
still speaking into the black.
Gone is the oyster-

white rocket. You can't
take it back.

Reaction

Chicago Pile-1

I wound through the gothic castle
                    buildings in the university of stained glass,
its windows open in early July

                    neutrally through metal frames
to allow in the sound of electric tools
                    biting around some white petunias

men handled with gloves like marble
                    sculptures of minor gods.
I crossed over the buried

                    reactor without thought, trying to learn
enough French to pass the language
                    of time: I remember some Sartre.

I finished a translation after coffee and pancakes
                    the morning of my birthday, then oiled my arms
in sunscreen and caught the bus

                    to the lake, that day a sheen of sealskin gray.
A lifeguard in an orange vest
                    had been cutting across the waves

in an aluminum boat when she started yelling
                    words at us through a megaphone,
but the wind ripped them out of her throat—

                    as if they were individual knots in a kite string
or the model numbers printed on an endoscope wire
                    you swallow like a pill to photograph your inner
                    folds,

the camera then cut out of you—
                        then the garble amplified angrier
as the glittered crests began to swell

                        faster over the sandbar, our legs
pegging us in the muck while the system
                        lit up in hexagons and hexagons

that rose to the waist and refused to be a mirror.
                        I scrawled in blue pen,
Dostoevsky ~~wrote~~ *had written,* "*If God* ~~does~~

                        did not exist, all would be permitted."
What is a peaceful objective? In the ground,
                        scientists embedded bars of graphite with an
                        idea,

as though a giant hand would lift one and rub the flesh
                        drawing of a person darker—adjusting
                        neutrons—
hatching a curve into the thigh. Goodyear Tire manufactured the
  balloon cloth

                        protecting the reaction in December 1942.
Students would have been stepping over the bundles
                        of ice, rehearsing tables, battles, phrases:

All would be permitted. An objective is a thought
                        not influenced by feeling. Control the chain.
That winter afternoon, the sun set early—as it does.

Repository

I.

I woke at 3 AM because my right ear itched, as though I'd been swimming or a friend had yelled a secret into my hair. I live in a city in the middle of the country. The red swirls of the worst storms moving over a map often miss the dot that represents where I live: the wooden fire escape off my kitchen that overlooks an alley of quick garages—I say quick because within days, a neighbor built one with a team of workers over the grass of his backyard—are a value of gray that reminds me of the moon. I live under the flight path of an international airport. Some evenings, in the dark of electrical wires and lampposts, I'll stand at the railing listening to dishes clatter in the sink of the apartment above me while I watch the yellow specks arrive overhead in a line—points moving as though in an argument together. They enlarge in the shape of tilted *X*s. I think about how I should count my credit card points, charge a flight to Albuquerque, then rent a car to Carlsbad, where my grandfather trained, and then to Alamogordo, where he also trained. I should study *Carlsbad* in my great aunt's handwriting in the little leather-bound book she kept of her nephew's addresses after he enlisted at seventeen. Her pen lingered on the tips of the *H* of his first name, marking the parallel lines of the letter that look like a sketch of a railroad track. I linger there too, as though the mark might mean something other than the fact that she thought about him. *I can't hear you,* my friend screamed in my ear at a party I went to in my early twenties. *I can't hear you.*

II.

It is from one hieroglyphic record that we know how ancient sailing is: a square sail indicates a ship from another land. From an out-of-print book, I learn *That no Greek or Latin map has survived of any that might have been drawn more than two thousand years ago is hardly to be wondered at.* Christian monks preserved early English poems—trees becoming Christ. In lettering the early songs by daylight, then candlelight, these monks happened to create an archive. The author writes, *It cannot be expected that they would have interested themselves in the technical equipment of sailors,* meaning, in sailing maps of the sea. I want to disappear into this information as though I'm the woman on the raft who appears on the water, from the water, to take the king's head onto her lap, wipe the blood from his eyes, and vanish. On Friday, there was an incident in the underground repository at the Waste Isolation Pilot Plant twenty-seven miles east of Carlsbad, New Mexico. Eleven personnel were working at the surface when the alarm triggered in the Central Monitoring Room. Contamination drifted across the countryside twenty-six miles west. The contaminated waste should be isolated from the biosphere until the risks posed by possible releases are acceptably small. In order to accomplish this, knowledge of the location and nature of the wastes must be maintained and passed on to future societies. The Great Pyramids are between four thousand and five thousand years old. A range of possible future societies may occur in the vicinity of the site throughout its regulatory period of ten thousand years. In ten thousand years, the axis of the Earth will point away from the North Star to a position midway between the bright stars Deneb and Vega.

III.

I never really believed my mother when she told me how she and her sister, who shared a bedroom in a postwar bungalow in North Jersey, turned out the light, pulled the sheets up to their chins, and said, *See you tomorrow,* one evening in October 1962 as though they might not. The scene that ends *Dr. Strangelove* replays only a handful of the atomic detonations we tested and filmed: I recognize a few by their shape, such as Baker, which we exploded underwater at Bikini Atoll. We buried tools and clothes from some of the 106 atomic bombs we exploded in the Pacific and the 911 atomic bombs we exploded in Nevada 2,150 feet below ground surface, into the Permian-age salt bedrock just within the perimeter of New Mexico. One June morning, after my summer class ended for the day, I entered the university library and crossed over the atrium, passing the escalator creating then flattening steps without anyone on them, and headed for the fire stairs located at the side of the building. I wanted some exercise after giving the midterm: watching scribbles, sighs, furrowed eyebrows. Were my students confused or concentrating? I opened the door to the fourth floor, and the book stacks I wanted were blocked off by translucent tarps. Industrial fans moved them gently. A taped-up sign explained how I could get to the other side, using cardinal directions: *Head to North stacks. Go down stairs. Head to South stacks.* Before we discovered the magnetic needle, sailors followed the sun by day and the stars by night for three thousand years. The whole northern quarter can be picked out by a brilliant group of seven stars—called the Bear, or the Plough—that neither rises nor sets. The stars circle round and round a point above your head.

IV.

Like asbestos, radioactive material collects in lung tissue. Unlike a cigarette, nothing you breathe in comes out. One argument made in the report issued by the Sandia National Laboratories in the early 1990s to consider how to mark the Waste Isolation Pilot Plant and warn future generations about drilling into it is that not only will our language, values, and even relationship to particular symbols reorient, but also the effects of being exposed to radiation can take years to appear. So we decided against an overstatement of a danger like "immediate death." In one sequence of proposed markings for the site, a child will first encounter the waste—symbolized by a trefoil. One can make a trefoil with a string by joining the ends of a knot before pulling it tight. This symbol appears in yellow on signs like the one fixed to the brick wall of my elementary school. I first remember noticing it during a game of four square, where you draw a kind of Punnett square with chalk and stand inside it with three other children, trying to trick each other into bouncing a rubber ball on a dividing line. I did not know what the three-paneled symbol meant, but it indicated something important about the building that made me glad someone was In Charge of These Things. After the drawing of the child that we will inevitably read as male touches the waste symbol, the trefoil transfers onto his chest—like armor. This causes the child to become special. Maybe he was sickly before encountering the symbol, unable to run as fast as the other children and quieter than they are. Now he will never be as he was before. He has a new kind of power no one else has. In the background of the drawing, trees appear. A sacred grove grows around him. We know the child will become an adult because he later stands taller in these trees—the symbol still on his chest. Flowers at his feet also indicate scale. Daisies or black-eyed Susans. An additional frame shows his body in death, the trefoil still on him. It splays over his ribs, like a soul.

V.

I like rainy June mornings where I sit by a half-open window in a long-sleeved shirt, feeling cold. What bothers me most about the Sandia Report on the Waste Isolation Pilot Plant is how it assumes there will be no human memory of radioactive material. I can't imagine what could happen—other than a nuclear event—that would restructure society, vaporize all museums, melt racks of data servers in buildings across the globe, and cause us to treat some landscapes as though we have never seen them before in seven thousand years, in a desert now a field on Earth where we are able to think about our relationship between where we stand, a cluster of cattle, and blossoms of beardtongue. The rock and water nearby may not look, feel, or smell unusual. But the site itself should announce, *Something made by humans is here.* A landscape of thorns. *Two vast and trunkless legs of stone.* Message kiosks will include languages of the United Nations—Arabic, English, Spanish, French, Russian, and Chinese—and of the largest group of Native Americans in the area: Navajo. A marker can be an effective warning if it survives, you can find it, its message reads as a warning, and this warning initiates appropriate action. At 23:14 Mountain Standard Time, there was an incident in the underground repository at the Waste Isolation Pilot Plant twenty-seven miles east of Carlsbad, New Mexico. At 16:35 the next day, the shelter-in-place order was lifted, and nonessential personnel were systematically released, building by building. Questioning attitudes are not welcomed by management: workers do not feel comfortable identifying issues like degraded equipment. An astronomical calendar will indicate when the site has closed: you can line up the angles of the star-rise of Sirius, Canopus, Arcturus, and Vega with the accompanying map. The URS Corporation, which currently owns the Nuclear Waste Partnership LLC that runs the Waste Isolation Pilot Plant, features an ethics page on their website. There is a photo of two men's hands cropped at the suit-sleeve—one in black, one in gray with a graphite-sheen to the weave—clasped in a handshake. *We are subject to the laws and regulations in each of the counties where we conduct business.* I like rainy June mornings where I sit by a half-open window in a long-sleeved shirt, feeling cold.

VI.

Plans indicate we will remove the existing buildings, parking lots, and roads to return the area to its previous condition. Maybe part of the main building holding the "hot cell" should remain. Future archeologists could study it. One of the facial expressions the Sandia Report suggests we carve into the marker looks like Edvard Munch's *The Scream*. We want faces that portray horror and sickness. We do not want these faces to be stolen and displayed in museums and private collections. Watch a face change for you, looking at something in the distance then smiling for you, as though a spotlight moved over the eyelids and chin. We assume human facial expressions are universal. *Were my students confused or concentrating?* A design itself conveys levels of information. This message is a warning about the danger. This is not a place of honor. This place is a message. It commemorates no highly esteemed deed.

We once considered ourselves a powerful culture.

White Sands Missile Range

New Mexico

I stand like a flag over my flesh.
          All around me, khaki-colored dirt
spots with pockets of yucca.

I am a cherry pit in a bowl
          between the mountains.
I think a cemetery will mushroom

around me in gum-colored stones,
          and I will read the names of the dead.
Instead, wind walls me up in debris

lifted from the atomic test site
          closed to visitors most days—unlike here.
This is a field. I expected placards

in sans serif font saying what
          saved these metal whales
from exploding in the sea

of sand. But a path snakes
          around them, and I push
my camera into my palm like an avocado.

I want to say ravens settle in the trees.
          I want to say *evening*. Miles off, a pilot
feathers the starling-egg sky

high on the wings of an F-16.
          What happens now? Fear is
fear. I'm standing in a field of warheads

all pointing in the same direction
      up at the sky. Let's go to the moon
in an empty tomb. Let's wait

like a mannequin with a bowl cut,
      and slide under lead
blankets into sleep. Let's not.

Song for Holding Tanks in a Vault

Las Conchas Fire, New Mexico

Smoke passes under the kitchen curtains—my body. My mood.
A ring of tar won't scrub from this mug. Water, water
scorched out of bark black as a wick bringing amber and chalk
light to me. An orange torch comes for the animal
under my house. Under my house, no cavern can hold you
alive forever. Nervous, your creator is humming.
I do not believe a concrete heaven, my animal of
Los Alamos, my animal exhaling threads of toxic
floss that thread through my lungs. Pilots training above me
in the desert air earned silver bomb rings. Red
fins, metallic tip. Tinnitus, piccolo
pitch, crest of a county-wide siren—my ears are splitting.
I'm not sick yet. But the pink land covers it all
like an infection. I shovel sand over you in my mind.
In my mind, you are dragging my body to the fire, bruises
printing my arms. I'm in my mind. This is
my mind. Get me away from the blood center
of a hibiscus. Get me away from the charm
of a bell. Everything is burning. This isn't hell.

Memory Mock-Up

I rode an elevator to Lookout Point. A shoebox factory
rippled the river and flung cotton strands of smoke into the sky.
In front of me, below the window, on a plastic model,
the factory did not exist. *Ignored* is not the word for the stars
obscured like pinholes in the cedar air. Or a satellite.
Or the cloth collar of the white shirt your lover threw over

a chair. Here are optics: a black bulb bluing your teeth.
And what do you say when you wake up
in a room rotating around you, *strange, strange,* until a voice
explains with the measuring tape of narrative, object
to object? I'm visiting this place. This place is my body.
And in the morning, the clematis clinging to the neighbor's fence

gleams inside its fuchsia petals, and I run
through the vines, to a brick tower with a ramp
where old men and women push themselves against metal frames
down to a van. Its engine rambles, and everyone is quiet.
I imagine poppy wallpaper wraps the walls of rooms, bodies
sleeping with black beads placed on the tongue. "There is a war going on,

you know." And I'm making a bridge out of toothpicks
and bone glue: triangle, triangle, take the weight. Yellow
joint. Take the pressure. Trust me. What is the name
of the river? Look out, I am wiping gesso on a canvas
with a wide, flat brush. What is the name of the space in the mind
of burned-out apartments, three in a row, hollow,

with a stench of singed mussel shells? Waiting with some children,
I believe in the structure that still stands, blackened, will always stand.
We chant: Someone had an idea. And we filled a cup with oil.
Someone had an idea. And we filled a cup with salt.
We lit it on fire, and we put it out. It is red today.
My neighbor washed all of her red linens, and on the line,

they signal a hurricane or an invasion. Her crimson
sheet screens the seed-pod husks,
sunflower heads burned out by the sun. A dress,
three shirts, and a pair of pants: red. Red. Pay attention.
In the twentieth century, an electric drum washing machine was invented
in Chicago, its inside coated in zinc. I *pliet* in front of the portal,

pulling a blanket out. Its folds spoon the shadows.
So. I rode an elevator to Lookout Point. I'm cold,
thinking about my bare bed, a map of my form below me,
my hands hovering over the compressed foam.
I think of a wound-up, tangled phone cord dangling
down the wall. And I'm in the kitchen I knew as a child,

the floor marked up near the oven. I genuflect in front of this
absent corner of mind. Why is today the day
for color, like the animated water, more orange than cardinal,
in *Impressionism Sunrise?* I wish it weren't a cliché to name it,
the paint quickly taking in light. When I feel light in my hair,
in an hour it's gone. Once upon a time, an old woman

left a bag of Empire apples on the landing of my apartment,
and I ate one, and slept and slept, and became her. When I woke, a mouth
pressed against my mouth. Once upon a time, in a city
garden, tomatoes were warmed inside to their jewels and spotted
the morning, like when you stand up too fast.
A storm was brewing in the scribbled clouds

pulling apart as though a brush wiped water across them.
Once upon a time, I stood in a glass tower, the sparkling cars
moving underneath me in an even pulse.
I rode an elevator to Lookout Point. And next to me,
as though I peered into a mirror, I saw a condemned bridge,
a prior bridge, rusted and not even particular. A year ago, this very view

of a factory that pulls water inside its walls, a motion I am
not supposed to see, did not exist. A year ago, these sparkling cars
crossed the shadow bridge, without warning, and continued over the river.

Song Pulled from a 1954 *National Geographic*

with wires, needles, or beads of radioactive gold

It isn't like the skin to choose transparency:
coffee too cool in a cup to blister the tongue.

When does the energy in your bones invite ghosts
to pick through your skull and touch the brain?

My coffee cools hardly hot into my palm.
Who knew the iron *Vs* of a linden leaf or dragonfly wing

could write through the skull and scratch the brain?
The material lifts lighter than a pencil scoring a game:

one for the iron veining your arm, a leaf, or the glassed wing of a fly.
Burn it longer than coal—more mixed in with the ash.

I won't watch it lift like a signature from a page.
Could a piano wire circle all the ships of the navy?

We burn coal and dream of more in the ash
like alchemists always almost making gold in a lab.

And a piano wire will hum and hum for the dead.
And a remote control will protect you from the self in the mirror.

One element is now another like gold grown in a lab:
I've seen the gapped bridge between an oil field and the sun.

We can control a substance remotely. Like a second self in a mirror,
no sound calls to you from within the walls.

The gap between an oil rig and the inexhaustible sun
closes with words: *isos* (same) and *topos* (place).

No smoke emerges from behind the concrete walls.
Sometimes, I sense the presence of forces, unheard and unseen

from a single place. *The same place.* How?
A beam of neutrons releases through an open lid.

Hold your breath against what you can't hear or see.
A doctor may ask you to drink one of the vials.

Through an open lid, a beam of neutrons will release.
The energy in my bones invites my ghosts in.

Let's wing the thing a doctor asks. Drink. Drink.
The body can be made again, transparent.

Declassified Test Film

They eat close to the surf,
laughing as water un-combs
plum threads
from a surface that flickers
quickly in and out of
sunflowers.

I wait for the sudden
sunset, tangerine, sun-
less as it blooms.
One of the soldiers has a question.
He rubs his nose with his thumb.
Is it that silver

speck up there?
He's in the cotton white
t-shirt you like to wear.
I fold your sleeves in a mess and press them
to my face—your stink
in the boat

seam of fabric.
"Where the Boys Are" by Connie Francis
drones from a radio speaker, her breath
mingling with the gold-
painted mesh.
They dig their feet in the sand

peaking here and there like buttercream.
Suddenly, the song
stupidly playing
breaks out
of shape, and everyone
flinches

then stares
right at the sky.

Yucca Flat

Nevada

We couldn't understand this location.
Three thousand feet above this spot the bomb will explode.
Try right clicking on the map.
An officer orders the infantry to move. The closest.

Directions. Las Vegas: seven hours, forty-six minutes. Bicycling.
I reach up.
Two hours, three minutes.
By car.

I rip the lens right out of the goggles.
It was a plastic lens.
The silence before the roar.
My hands over my eyes.

In the flash
I could see the bones of my fingers.

The Angels Sing

The plot thickens: we've started a band
in the old glassworks factory, where bottles in a white
        window painted shut still lip the fire from the sun
& blame the field for being sold, for being blood

        for the pudding & the cuckoo for the cage & the cardboard
slat folding into the box that cradles your fetish—
        we know about it. We remember the grove moving
with starlings that dropped all around you

        to eat from the grass one afternoon along the river.
It would only have taken one switch when the B-52
        crashed to waken the wires in the metal
vessel and blow up North Carolina. Chance is our band

of relationships landing us alive. Hark, the herald mating
        game: *a-a-a-a-a-lleluia.*

Pool

Across the street two Santas have been smoking for twenty minutes.
　　　　I am carrying a pound of hard green pears. I have nothing to say.
The community swimming pool, glittering in the ground, is covered
　　by a tarp.
　　　　The underworld has been sealed. And all I have is my body

to carry and feed a pound of pears—it is like having nothing,
　　　　draping curtains pulled from a box over myself.
The underworld is sealed up, and this is all I have: my body
　　　　to clothe and walk to the bank under the black trees and sky

draping starkness, this pulled curtain, everywhere. In a box I will put myself:
　　　　we only live on in the memories of three generations, I've heard,
clothed and walking outside while we move in the wet black trees, the sky,
　　　　being within them as ourselves, the way six people can step inside
　　　　　　a sheet of cut paper.

We only live on in the memories of three generations—I heard this
　　　　from a man lecturing the branches of an ash tree—
being in them, ourselves this way. When people exist in names marked on
　　paper
　　　　all each person has is their own body and the trick itself: being.

A filthy man lectures the raining branches of an ash tree
　　　　while two Santas smoke. Twenty minutes pass.
All I can say I have is a body and the trick itself: being,
　　　　until the community's swimming pool, glittering in the morning,
　　　　　　opens.

The Atomic Bomb of Operation Crossroads Speaks

Bikini Atoll, 1946

This was not
my idea.
The fliers elected
to paint a
woman's lips
on me. Kiss.
Kiss.
Naval
carriers
wait in the
lagoon. Empty.
I am their
supervisor.
I make men
drop white mice
with bare hands
into a
cage. I make
hills of water
crinkle like
cabbage.
"Bikini
target" sounds
like it means
cunt. I've heard
that said all
over my
shell. Inside,
I am time.
How should I
unstring these
clouds? Easy
now. Easy.

Oath Inked in the Air with a Crow-Quill Pen

After unhooking from a chain and after
its hinge fused the hemispheres,
what looks like a balloon
was driven off by a shirtless boy—

the metallic pit compressed inside of it.
Pilots signed the curve like a cast: *Here's to you.*
They wished themselves all over the shell.
Because of crows fighting on the roof

of my apartment
in a city in the United States,
I'm going to make a promise in ink
that has an idea of a crow in it—

the way history becomes a diagram
promising a room
where the windows keep shifting positions.
The crows mark me

with their black feathers.
Above my kitchen, some military jets
cross out the clouds
for an air show. It's August again.

A woman becomes a silhouette.
I rubbed the rays—
albumen strings through my fingers.
Her silk textile has been tattooed

in blood ladders up her back,
and I have taken her
though she turned away
from the photographer and closed her eyes.

Did she think she gave her exposed self
to a doctor instead of the blink
a lens catches from the light
reflecting off of skin? I am still

moving through this.
Let the dew point be my witness
that I do not know
what it means to look at anything—

like prints of fruit crate art
where there is a griffin
guarding three oranges and decide *why*,
its lion tail curled in an *O*.

O as the gray pipe of the security camera
fastened to the corner
of my building is my witness,
I will never be able to do

anything but give you an image
of your own shadow stretched out emptily
over the ground.
I am almost here now.

The shadow is an airplane
arriving low over a road
that converges with another road,
splits two fields,

then opens to a town
dotting a shoreline with peaked roofs.
I only have a copy
of this view

extending to the sea—
the sea stippled like silverpoint,
the oldest way to strike out a surface:
glue mixed with ground bone.

Marie Curie

When our baskets filled, I would step
                off the boat and balance in my palm
an apple finer than the others—cold
                skin that cracked under my teeth.
There was one dream: nationalism,

                the exposed nerves of beet roots
tangled in bullock carts
                moving slowly toward the factory chimney
choughing its thing at the sky.
                Some sentences escape me.

I take the sun, and I throw it.
                I remember the stoop-shouldered men
tracking equations the professor's fingers
                tapped across the chalkboard.
I take the sun, and I throw it

                in an attic like a servant's room
warmed by a skylight
                topping the middle-class house. No heat,
no water—but a kitchen chair
                and petroleum lamp that I covered

with a two-penny shade. I would wash
                my dress in a pail and mend its hem.
When I wanted a treat,
                I would walk through the Latin Quarter
to the creamery and eat two eggs.

When I came back to myself, I would ask
why I fainted, my stomach
            round with radishes and cherries.
In this atmosphere of wrinkled linen,
            I would wait for the poplar leaves—

my window shut tight to their branches.
            I would dress myself in navy
for him, my blouse in robin egg stripes.
            My partner's jacket boxed his torso
in a cut ten years old. We owned two bicycles.

            We celebrated up the boulevard Saint-Michel,
watching the city pass us from the top of a bus,
            our faces pinked by the sun.
And we lunched on bread and peaches,
            slept in a room with faded wallpaper,

and slept through the night. He had no sense
            of time: a few thousand pedal strokes,
then we arrived at a pond grown in with grass
            where he gathered irises and water lilies
for me while I slept. Once, he dropped a frog,

            light-bodied, that peed into my hand.
And in our little flat, I would peel parsnips
            and onions for the noon meal.
When I woke with the autumn light,
            I left for our shed

in my lab coat without a hat or a scarf.
            I met the wagon usually loaded with coal

in the street that morning.
                              I touched the cloth of one sack & cut the strings
with a bread knife & opened its mouth

                              & put my hands deep
into the ore, the pitchblende mixed with pine needles
                              from Bohemia. It was like creating nothing
out of nothing, all summer
                              in the shed without cupboards:

particles in glass tubes on shelves
                              we nailed into the wall,
bluish outlines glowing like what
                              we couldn't describe.
I sat in the dark,

                              in the violet activity, and watched.
As a child, I would dig up mud
                              with the tines of a fork
and form the dirt into huts,
                              pushing windows in with my fingers.

There is an actor among us
                              that lives in the earth
and in the air. In the evening,
                              we would return exhausted,
our arms prickling in red veins.

                              Our best disguise is an appearance.
I would sit barefoot on our front step,
                              scraping it with my shoe.
I was loosening sand from the toe.
                              I also wanted a child.

Field Notes: Birds

Birds of the Nevada Test Site, 1963

Scientists named the first test in this area
Able—sometimes a diamond replaces a heart.
Scorched vegetation soon greens with thistle.

In winter, the house finch feeds on it in flocks.
In May, I caught sight of an osprey circling
sage the disturbance scattered with fire. To the south,

I saw a roadrunner nest! Structured with snakeskin
and pinfeathers, it cradled four eggs
in the engine fan of an abandoned plane.

In September, we exploded a tunnel in a drift
mined into a mesa. Green heron.
One specimen: the bird sick and unable

to fly in October. November. *Western
Grebe*: I lifted a sick one from the road,
like an empty pillow case. And then?

The degree of disturbance decreases as the radius
extends. I've felt the seismic shocks.
But I found Jerusalem cricket shells in the pellets

dropped by migrating hawks. See those two lakes
and the flats sloping around them? Mourning doves,
I would guess five thousand, would come to the water,

skimming it in the evening. And in the heat
of midsummer, many would cool in the caves.
Sing the tune without the words. I? I

recorded thousands of them from the access
road. *Swallow. Crow. Magpie.* Collection
records: *none.* I've even seen ravens

here in the sun, appearing like paper
cutouts on utility poles. *I've heard it*
in the chillest land - / And on the strangest sea -

My present study is limited by these boundaries.

Personal History

I'm supposed to be sliding
my numb toes into boots,
zipping them up my calves
to bring the mail in. Three
lemons rot in a gray bowl.
I used to write letters to both
sets of grandparents, my pilot
grandfather responding sometimes.
During my "tomboy" phase,
he would try to teach me tennis
in a park in Vermont—a hornet
pausing around me while I swung,
the brim of my Bulls cap
shadowing my eyes. The apostrophe
of a stinger would find my brother,
his ankles—how he would run away
from the empty swings, crying.
My grandfather told him once: *to escape,*
fly so high, the enemy can't read you,
the clouds wound in balls
of cotton candy, the drop
tickle in the stomach, the lift—
he hardly spoke to us
the rest of the afternoon.
So my brother and I threw hot dog buns
at geese, their toes dragging
fans through the water that became pins
of light & the rest of the story is like satin
stitches that cover a background in lines.

Tucked into black paper tabs,
a photo of an atomic cloud
marks the page of an album.

I guess it's OK now, he said, meaning
giving it away. It will not make you
close your eyes. It does not match
the famous image—fireball
ballooning up, top split from the stem.
Our photo shows an intact, darker
column of breath—blink,
swallow—sooner. *Tick, tick, tick.*
Whose? Another official shot.
I imagine a page of language
that appears to be woven
from platinum—each verb glinting.
The surface itself would be an excerpt
knifed from the hem of a priest's robe.
A priest's body is on loan
in one museum, the placard explaining
how under the lid of the sarcophagus
a scribe copied the glyphs of a prayer
too old for him to understand:
vertical bars patterned with eyes,
another line like a fret glued
to a guitar. Did the garble
protect this body from history?
Is that what language does?
I kneeled at the bottom of its glass
case and stared. Here are the chapped feet.

Dream of the Morning Before It Split Open

I almost see your thumb
following the groove
like a river on an atlas.

The plane won't be parked long.
You chip a stone out
of the tire, your mind

waking up as light
patterns the palms.
Men peer from the slits

of tents as though through ash,
their eyes opening
in a pan of photographic fixer.

What will you see from the bottom
bulb of glass? The warp of August
sun metalling the waves?

You turn toward your name
as though your father called you
back. You step under the wing of it.

Hiroshima

from John Hersey's Hiroshima

For a few seconds or minutes, he went out of his mind.
      Dark clothes absorbed and conducted it to the skin.
He noticed a pumpkin roasted on the vine.
      The fire was coming closer on the wind.

From east to west, the city toward the hills,
      everything whiter than any white I'd seen.
No sound of planes. The morning still.
      To the south: docks and an island-studded sea.

Just as I turned my head away from the windows,
      the bottle of blood crashed against one wall.
In the basement vault, the X-ray plates were exposed.
      Water the size of marbles began to fall.

Because of an irresistible urge to hide,
      foliage seemed like the cool core of life.

Elegy for the Human Shadow Etched in Stone

Hito Kage No Ishii, steps of Sumitomo Bank, Hiroshima

Archive of a person, you cross your legs
below the sun. It looks like a bundle of linens
climbs the stairs above you
daily as a bell pulled in a tower.
Early enough for an errand, carrying papers
folded up in your hand, you once moved through the air
graying the road in half of a grace
held by a sheen of ox-blood leaves.
In the muscle of the stomach where worry is swallowed,
jasmine began to cool. Can I call it light,
knowing what came? Kettle scorched,
lips and throat gone before calling out then
marbling in a pattern you might cure with balm
nightly until your eyes would cataract into Jupiter pupils,
open as an owl's—opening—opening.
Particles jump out of thought:
quills of light, heels of molten glass
ripped up from the ground by wind.
Someone else shielded in a room underground
took a breath, then another breath—
umbra of gums bleeding under the teeth.
Vapor is a value. Suddenly, you were every-
where when the bank door unbolted,
X-marks tracked like minutes marked in dust.
Your mind webbed with heat in one second.
Zone of noon. Stolen form. I can't name you.

Notes

My grandfather's possible involvement in the Nagasaki mission has remained a mystery.

~

The epigraph comes from Gertrude Stein's *Tender Buttons.*

"First Thing" (p. 5) incorporates details from a passage of Richard B. Frank's *Downfall: The End of the Imperial Japanese Empire* (New York: Random House, 1999) excerpted in *The Manhattan Project,* ed. Cynthia C. Kelly (New York: Black Dog & Leventhal, 2007).

"The Sun Rising, Pacific Theatre" (p. 6) borrows "The Sun Rising" from John Donne.

The "Exposure" sequence (pp. 17–29) borrows from accounts of survivors of the Hiroshima and Nagasaki bombings (*hibakusha*). The people whose voices appear in these poems are Kosaku Okabe, Sakae Hosaka, Teiichi Teramura, Kiyoko Sato, Akira Nagasaka, Misue Sagami, Asae Miyakoshi, Fumiko Nonaka, Machiyo Kurokawa, Hiroshi Shibayama, Masae Kawai, Sumiko Umehara, Shige Hiratsuka, Sachiko Masaki, Tadaomi Furuishi, Kayoko Satomi, Michiko Fujioka, and Akihiro Takahashi. Their accounts appear in *Hibakusha: Survivors of Hiroshima and Nagasaki,* trans. Gaynor Sekimori, (Tokyo: Kōsei Publishing Co., 1986). The Bashō haiku is quoted from *The Essential Haiku: Versions of Bashō, Buson, & Issa,* trans. Robert Hass (Hopewell, N.J.: Ecco Press, 1994).

"Guilt Offering" (p. 33) alludes to the biblical scapegoat and quotes as its epigraph a phrase from Leviticus 16:22 (*Tanakh,* new JPS version).

"Cloud Cover" (p. 34) borrows from the article "Weather Fights and Works for Man" published in the December 1943 issue of the *National Geographic,* pp. 631–60.

"Parachute" (p. 35) borrows from John Ruskin's *The Elements of Drawing* originally published in 1904 (Mineola, N.Y.: Dover Publications, Inc., 1971). The epigraph of the poem quotes Assen Jordanoff's *Flying and How to Do It* (New York: Grosset & Dunlap, 1932).

"'Mike' Test" (p. 46) borrows a sentence from Declassified U.S. Nuclear Test Film #56 ("Enewetak Cleanup," n.d., YouTube).

"H-Bomb" (p. 48) borrows from Declassified U.S. Nuclear Test Film #12 ("Operation Ivy, Parts 1 and 2," 1952, YouTube) and from Google Maps.

"Fallout" (p. 50) borrows from Declassified U.S. Nuclear Test Film #12 ("Operation Ivy, Parts 1 and 2," 1952, YouTube).

"Starfish Prime Pantone-mime" (p. 51) alludes to the name of the hydrogen bomb ("Starfish Prime") shot into space on July 9, 1962. The poem borrows Pantone colors.

"Repository" (pp. 57–62) borrows from the Brookings Institution's article, "50 Facts About U.S. Nuclear Weapons," https://www.brookings.edu/50 -facts-about-u-s-nuclear-weapons/; the report prepared by Sandia National Laboratories, "Expert Judgment on Markers to Deter Inadvertent Human Intrusion into the Waste Isolation Pilot Plant" (https://prod.sandia.gov/ techlib-noauth/access-control.cgi/1992/921382.pdf, printed in November 1993); Percy Shelley's poem, "Ozymandias"; E. G. R. Taylor's *The Haven-Finding Art: A History of Navigation from Odysseus to Captain Cook* (New York: American Elsevier Publishing Company, 1971); the "Ethics" page of the URS Corporation's website (urs.com); and the U.S. Department of Energy Office of Environmental Management's Accident Investigation Report, "Phase I: Radiological Release Event at the Waste Isolation Pilot Plant on February 14, 2014" (April 2014, http://www.wipp.energy.gov/Special/ AIB_Final_WIPP_Rad_Release_PhaseI_04_22_2014.pdf).

The Las Conchas Fire ("Song for Holding Tanks in a Vault," p. 67) threatened the Los Alamos National Laboratory.

"Song Pulled from a 1954 *National Geographic*" (p. 70) borrows from "Man's New Servant, the Friendly Atom," *National Geographic* (January 1954, p. 71–90).

"Yucca Flat" (p. 74) borrows from an interview with Doug Wood, a photographer of Lookout Mountain Labs who filmed one of the atomic detonations at the Nevada Test Site in 1951, as well as from Google Maps.

Operation Crossroads ("The Atomic Bomb of Operation Crossroads Speaks," p. 77) was a series of atomic explosions the United States conducted at Bikini Atoll (Marshall Islands) in 1946. Rita Hayworth's photograph was painted on the nose of one of the bombs (in Test Able) without her permission.

"Marie Curie" (p. 84) borrows from *Madame Curie*, a biography by Eve Curie originally published in 1937 (New York: Pocket Books, 1946).

"Field Notes: Birds" (p. 87) borrows from *Birds of the Nevada Test Site* published in the Brigham Young University Science Bulletin's Biological Series (volume III, number 1) in June 1963 and Emily Dickinson's "'Hope' is the thing with feathers." Able was the name of the first test of Operation Ranger conducted on U.S. soil on January 27, 1951.

"Hiroshima" (p. 92) borrows from John Hersey's issue-length article for the August 31, 1946, *New Yorker*, published as a volume by Alfred A. Knopf later that year.

"Elegy for the Human Shadow Etched in Stone" (p. 93) is an elegy for the person who left the shadow on the steps of Sumitomo Bank, Hiroshima, 850 feet from the bomb's hypocenter.

Acknowledgments

I am grateful to the editors of the following journals where these poems first appeared, at times as earlier versions:

The Adroit Journal: "Marie Curie"

Another Chicago Magazine: "Field Notes: Birds"

Believer: "H-Bomb"

Birmingham Poetry Review: excerpts from "Exposure"

Blackbird: "Dream of the Morning Before It Split Open" "Hypothesis: An Interview," and "Negative Peeled from a Cardboard Album"

The Blueshift Journal: "The Muse Appears in My Kitchen"

Connotation Press: "Fallout" and "Reef"

Court Green: "Cloud Cover," "Dream of Taking the Hypoxia Altitude Test in a Metal Bird," and "Yucca Flat"

Crab Orchard Review: "Starfish Prime Pantone-mime"

Gulf Coast: "Nagasaki" and "Oxygen Mask"

Jet Fuel Review: "Oath Inked in the Air with a Crow-Quill Pen"

Kenyon Review: "Repository"

Kettle Blue Review: "Airman on the Ground"

Memorious: "Song for Holding Tanks in a Vault"

Narrative: "Reaction"

New England Review: "Wilderness Road"

New Old Stock: "Elegy for the Human Shadow Etched in Stone" and "Guilt Offering"

New Yorker: "The Sun Rising, Pacific Theatre"

Pinwheel: "Declassified Test Film," "Hawk Parable," and "Song Pulled from a 1954 *National Geographic*"

POETRY: "First Thing"

Poetry International: "Parachute"

Poetry Northwest: "Hiroshima"

Prairie Schooner: "Pool"

South Dakota Review: "Memory Mock-Up"

Tupelo Quarterly: excerpts from "Exposure"

upstreet: "On the Hawk that Crossed my Path in a Dystopian Landscape"
   and "White Sands Missile Range"
Zócalo Public Square: "Personal History"

"'Mike' Test" first appeared on the Academy of American Poets website
("Poem-a-Day," 2014). "H-Bomb" was reprinted in *Best American Experimental
Writing 2015* (Wesleyan University Press). "H-Bomb" and "The Sun Rising,
Pacific Theatre" are included in the directory of the public art piece, the
Telepoem Booth, a 1970s phone booth where one can dial-a-poem.

I'm indebted to Oliver de la Paz for selecting this manuscript, to the
University of Akron Press, especially Mary Biddinger and Amy Freels,
and to a number of generous readers; thank you to Srikanth (Chicu)
Reddy, Shara McCallum, Diane Seuss, Stanley Plumly, Fanny Howe,
Robert Hass, and Jennifer Ashton. Gratitude to Yaddo, the Vermont
Studio Center, Ragdale, Sewanee, the Kenyon Review Writers Workshop,
and the University of Illinois-Chicago Graduate College for the support
to finish this book. Many thanks to David Baker, Michael Collier, Brianna
Noll, Jenn Hawe, Susan Steinberg, Tom March, Carol Maldow, Elizabeth
Jacobson, Jenny George, Sarah Sillin, Corinna McClanahan Schroeder,
Lucy Biederman, Laura Deffley, Heather Blain Vorhies, Deanna Boulard,
Chris Messenger, Rania Abouzeid, Dale Megan Healey, Doron Langberg,
Elizabeth Lechner, Jordan Young, Peter Buchanan, Jennifer Perrine,
Heather Brown, Kendra DeColo, Christina Stoddard, and to my colleagues
and community at New Mexico Highlands University. Thank you, Arik
Lubkin, for being my reader and champion. Thank you to my family, near
and far, especially my parents, Dan Mills and Gail Skudera. Thank you
to all of my friends: my community in Chicago, where this book began,
and in Santa Fe, where it found its finish.

This book is dedicated to Arik and to my parents.

Photo: Arik Lubkin

Tyler Mills is the author of two books of poems, *Hawk Parable* (winner of the 2017 Akron Poetry Prize) and *Tongue Lyre* (winner of the 2011 Crab Orchard Series in Poetry First Book Award). Her poems have appeared in *The New Yorker*, *The Guardian*, and *Poetry*, and her essays have appeared in *AGNI*, *Copper Nickel*, and *The Rumpus*. The recipient of residencies from Yaddo, Ragdale, and the Vermont Studio Center, and scholarships/fellowships from Bread Loaf and Sewanee, the Chicago native is an assistant professor at New Mexico Highlands University, editor-in-chief of *The Account*, and a resident of Santa Fe, NM.